Twelve Paths to Power: The Art of Mastering Self

DeShawn Kenner

ISBN: 0989785416
ISBN-13: 978-0989785419

Layout by Sarah Anne Hubbard

Kenner Publishing
Lindenhurst, New York

Printed in the U.S.A.

DEDICATION

For those who know there is so much more to the self and
living, than currently meets the eye.

CONTENTS

He who knows not and knows not that he knows not is simple...disregard him.

He who knows not and knows he knows not is foolish...teach him.

He who knows not but believes he knows is dangerous...stay away from him.

He who knows but knows not that he knows is asleep...awaken him.

He who knows and knows he knows is awake...follow him.

~Ancient Egyptian Proverb

DeShawn Kenner

Introduction

The person who knows their self will know everyone else.
~old proverb

We live in a time that is saturated with different organized beliefs, cultures, ideas, and philosophies. A person can be born and indoctrinated with a way of life that they don't believe in wholeheartedly and not even be aware of it. You may feel some type of way about countless things and not understand why. Simply put you may not know how to feel what you really feel. You only go by what someone else or some other standard has set for you to feel. It can be hard for a person to know who they truly are with so much outside interference. Lots of people pass away with a concocted fake identity of self, never expressing who they authentically were; just leaving behind distorted views, illusions, and facades.

Anyone who aims to be a game changer in life must know what they stand for. Only the person with the greatest understanding of oneself in any and all aspects of existence will be able to obtain the greatest amount of peace, pleasure, and power. It does not matter the religion, continent, state, city, town, color, height, weight, gender, race, or politics; even though there is only one true race, the human race. The world will be at your mercy.

What is required is maturity. The Maturity to assimilate, absorb, and accept the truths of who you are. Recognize the natural strength that you possess, the real you. People tend to associate the past and history to who they or who we are now. Most of us are caught up in outdated traditions and beliefs that are irrelevant to what's going on now.

At some point in history at any given time, there has to be a beginning, a baseline, an era, or an age. It is up to the person or people who decide where or what the beginning is and in what direction they will go. In the same manner a person can have a beginning without yielding to the beliefs, traditions, and goals of the past. Whether it is the thesis meets the antithesis equals the synthetic new, or just the syncretic cultural melting pot view, start by asking yourself who am I, the real I?

These next twelve paths will lead you to the ultimate power; the knowledge, and truth of you. The journey to self is not an easy path. There is no room for a weak mindset; it requires perseverance, tolerance, patience, mental concentration, and durability; just to name a few. Before I end this introduction, I will tell you something you must not do, on any of these paths, you must not fear! You can never find your true self if you take fear with you on this quest.

This quest also consists of courage, humility, and realness. You will need the courage to get through the dangers on these paths. You will need humility because there will be certain parts of the journey that you will not be able to learn from or pass unless you are humble enough to embrace and accept the truths revealed to you. You have to be real with yourself, only then can you recognize the real you, and reveal it to yourself. You will have to search the highest of heights and the lowest of the bottoms of all hells, the heights of all heavens, the bottoms of the seas, and the top of the skies, all four corners of the world, and the universes which reside in you. I commend you for picking up this book and deciding to take on these paths, which says something about you all by itself.

You may just be built for the mission at hand. Just stay in accordance with the tips that I have aforementioned. You will reach great understandings of who you really are. Each level of understanding is a level of power. I wish you the best on your quest, let us begin.

1st Path: Be Honest with Yourself

Stop lying to yourself; if you lie to yourself it will be easy for others to lie to you. ~DeShawn Kenner

The first path entails that you do not lie to yourself. If you don't think you lie to yourself then you are lying to yourself at this very moment. This road is hard to travel because a great deal of people will find it rather difficult to stop the lies. If a person is excessively lying to oneself it creates a mind state of delusion. Once a person becomes delusional in many cases they start to believe their own lies, once this happens the fantasy begins. When one begins to live in a fantasy world (mainly who you think you are), naturally your true self rebels against this mentality. The true self knows the fantasy has no real substance and what has no substance in essence is empty. The two main parts of you are the internal (your spirit/personality) and external you (the body). Your body is made up of the same physical elements as the physical world. The internal and external you while independent of each other, are very much connected. I need you to view the body as a machine, a sophisticated vehicle nonetheless, but a machine. Where you are born into it, grow with it, and you learn how to use the body and all of its senses in many different ways over the course of time. The body is like any other vehicle with a driver, your spirit. If the vehicle is in gear it can move on its own or even on autopilot, where it will follow a set pattern regardless if it is the right course or not. As I stated in the introduction we are all born into certain beliefs and set patterns. Like autopilot that is what we run off of, that is the course that our external self follows, even when it does not feel right. When you do not feel right about something, it is your real self trying to take charge but somehow we have become stuck on autopilot, and are flying in the wrong direction.

We do so even when it is the way we really do not want to go. In order to loosen the hold that the autopilot of traditions and delusions has on you, you must stop lying to yourself. Do not allow others to lie to you either. However it will continue to be a simple task for others to deceive you as long as you keep casting hypnotic spells on yourself.

Many people have trouble sleeping and concentrating; always have anxiety, and depression. These people live a lot of lies and have not confronted them. You can lie to other people but when you try to run game on yourself, the inner self knows deep down which causes the inner conflict. You are the one person you should never try to get over on, this is a problem because you have flipped on your closest ally for no good reason, you. When you stop lying to yourself it brings about clarity and freedom which gives you strength and power.

As with myself, I will be real with you and myself at the same time. At times I can be arrogant and self absorbed. I know I'm not the most physically handsome male that has ever existed and at times my attitude stinks. However I know I am not the most unattractive either, and at other times my attitude is optimistic and pleasant. It's actually often more optimistic and pleasant than I care to admit. Beauty is in the eye of the beholder, meaning beauty is seen many different ways according to the individual viewing it. Not lying to self can be a challenge because of all the different external expectations and images that we are overwhelmed with. Once one can stop the lies or at least slow them down tremendously, you will feel energy and power return to you. The lies also extend into emotions, when you are feeling scared, nervous, happy, loving, hateful, jealous, and can't admit it; you will be uncomfortable, because you are not allowing yourself to deal with or fully recognize the feeling. This will keep you in an unbalanced state of being. Once you have gotten self lies under control and start getting rid of them, you should have enough strength to enter into the next path. This next path is just as if not more treacherous than the first.

2ⁿᵈ Path: Interrogation

Turn the bright light on yourself for questioning. ~Deshawn Kenner

Interrogation is a very important road, because after you have slowed down and stopped the lies to self, real work can begin. If I compared what we are doing to surgery, the first path would be the anesthesia, and interrogation would be the scalpel that makes the incision to see what is really going on inside of you. The difference between an interview and an interrogation is simple but clear. Interviews are about fact finding and personal perspectives. Whereas interrogation is solely about getting to the bottom line, the truth. Nothing else is more important than the truth in an interrogation; likewise this path is crucial in self discovery, as they all are. When you have stopped lying to yourself, it will be time to start telling yourself the truth. You must know the truth about you, who you really are, and what you are really about. You unlearn what other people have told you about yourself, what you have assumed about yourself, and how any society and all its various belief systems and traditions have labeled you. You are searching for the real driver of the sophisticated machine we call a body. The you that evaluates the thoughts of the brain and sits behind the curtain we call a mind, that is who you must go back to. How do you begin to interrogate yourself for the truth? As with anything else you start small and work your way up to bigger business. I have a list of startup questions for those who don't have a clue on where to begin. I mentioned this in 'No More Mistakes" you can start with easy self facts: gender, age, race, nationality, height, weight, mother, father, family members, like & dislikes, favorite color, etc. You must know the basic facts about yourself before you can move on to tougher issues. Next comes a little more in depth questions like are you religious or spiritual, do you believe in God, Allah, Buddha, Elohim, or believe in a Most High as a force that humans cannot describe? Understand that every walk of life has smart people that can logically make a case or a reasonable argument for why their belief or ideas are the most rational, with or without concrete evidence. So why should not your own personal views count for something. After all you are living the human experience, so never invalidate yourself, your thoughts, or your own perspective of the world or you.

When interrogating yourself know that regardless what answers and truths you discover, realize, or accept, nobody will know them but you. If you want to be cliché', it is between you and your maker. Although you consider yourself a tough as nails type of person, which may be true, you may embrace the fact that there have been times in your life where you were a coward, lived in fear, or just did not do the right thing at the time you were supposed to. Understanding these things is not to belittle yourself, but to help bring you full circle with self. Please acknowledge the truth that there are two sides to all things. A hot to a cold, a negative to a positive, a day to a night, recognizing the strong and weak sides of yourself strengthens you as an individual. These acknowledgments make you conscious of what you need to do to better yourself. You see the things you need to work on in regards to maturing yourself so that certain negative things that you could have prevented in the past never happen again, which is evolution of self.

There are millions of people walking around miserable, depressed, and sad just because they are in denial about who they really are. For example think of all the homosexuals that have lived in secret because of fears, family, and society expectations, etc. All the interracial couples that are hidden because the disappointment one's family might feel towards the union, even risking abandonment. Win, lose, or draw another or others opinions should never have that much leverage over you, to the point you feel oppressed or trapped. It does not matter who it is because your life is yours as long as you are not aggressively or violently imposing physical or mental harm on another. Pursue your happiness, manifest your destiny.

There are countless young people who degrade
their own intelligence and maturity levels trying
to fit in with the crowds. They cannot even begin
to comprehend the level that they are truly on; it
may be plain old inexperience or just not
accepting the superior minds that they possess.
There are tons of people who grow but never
reach their maximum potential, because they
lived in fear of being honest with themselves.
They could never interview let alone interrogate
themselves for uncut truth. Make no mistake
about it, just because a person has a high IQ does
not mean they can't live in fear. Think about how
a nerd is portrayed as timid, an insecure person in
comparison to the airhead but tough jock.

I think that is a terrible stereotype because the
more you know and understand, the more
empowered and confident one becomes. Not
knowing and uncertainty keeps a person off
balance and unsure naturally. How does fear play
on a Wiseman's wisdom? I know this is tough;
we all start out with hard heads but seek to end

up with an open mind. The mind cannot open up if it is soaking in fear regardless of how genius the mind is. How do you rid yourself of fear? You don't, you realize that it naturally exists like any other element, such as oxygen, carbon dioxide, gold, zinc, hydrogen, etc. We allow fear to control nothing, but seek to use it as a resource like plutonium, petroleum, or crude oil; it can be a fuel for your vehicle. There are enlightened people who already know this truth.

National governments and religions, use fear as a weapon to control massive populations. whether a person fears being killed, going to prison, being stripped of material gains, or going to hell, fear is used as leverage. If someone else has leverage which puts you off balance, you can never be aligned with yourself. Interrogate yourself fearlessly. Find your balance, however be careful. Always being careful is just watching what you do, your method of approach. A method I have suggested of discovering self was to start small and work your way big. You can also start with hard questions and work your way down.

Whatever way makes you comfortable is what I recommend you do. This interrogation could take hours, days, months, years, or simply be an ongoing process because it is possible to discover something new about yourself and the world each day. You should interrogate yourself, by yourself, so that you are left alone for intense questioning. This may make you laugh, cry, angry, happy, ashamed, proud, hateful, loving, regretful, or justified. However in the end you should feel closer to you, more in tune with yourself. Interrogation pushes you to reflect on your life, times, and actions. Interrogations bring out the truth about you, shows who you really are, and what you are really about. It reveals you in your truest nature, so take a look at yourself, do not resist you in any way. Embrace you in every way, the good, the bad, and the ugly. This brings us to the next path.

3rd Path: Embrace You

You should always be at home with yourself! ~DeShawn Kenner

Once you have realized ways, actions and even thoughts that you have, you additionally may come to know that there are things that you do not like about yourself. Despite all that, those characteristics are all yours. It's almost like having a drug addict for a parent or close relative, no matter how much they have hurt you with their addictions, you are still related to them. No matter how much you pretend like you don't know them or disown them, that does not change the fact that they are your biological family with whom you share the same blood and DNA. But in this case it is YOU, your closest family member, how do you even consider turning your back on yourself? That is very unreasonable and unproductive, because if you are to be the authentic you, you must embrace yourself completely.

It is like ripping a dollar bill in half, the appearance of it may be altered and worthless in that condition, however to bring value back to that dollar you must reconnect it. Usually when people reconnect torn paper bill money, they use scotch tape, because it is see through and is an easy and gentle mending method for the bill. The tape will only work and be allowed on real money, not half of a real bill and half of a Parker's Brothers Monopoly buck, it won't work because the money is not all the way real. I realize we live in an age where most things are electronic and digital, so I'll say this only your code will get you into your bank account. Regardless if you don't like your account numbers, only your code will access you to yours. Whatever you don't agree with about yourself you need to correct, because it is you. It's a serious task, so you will need to put yourself under construction, and let the rebuilding begin. See yourself as your own house, no matter how beat up it may get with endless repairs, that is your house and you have the responsibility of maintaining it. It is your dwelling where you live, and if you do not take care of it, it will fall apart, and you will have nothing. The work is never easy but it is always worth it. Once you have embraced yourself, you can strip anything off of you that you don't like, and put on what needs to be there. Dress yourself mentally, physically, and spiritually in the manner that most represents who the real internal you or 'I' is. There are so many different sides to a person that if you do not pay close attention to yourself consciously, you could overlook detailed, intricate, important parts of who you are. It is like the person that does not realize that they have outgrown their old shoe size, yet still walks around in the old stretched out now too small shoe, and wonders why their feet hurt. You are the ruler of yourself no one has to elect you for that, you are born into your own body and your life is yours. It is to be cherished, respected, loved, protected, challenged, and matured and not experienced whereas an experienced person is educated on a whole different higher level. You may have heard about people, places, and things yet have seen nothing, been nowhere, or have not talked to anybody. The real education lies within experience. You can read a driver's manual and know what all the signs and signals mean, however actually getting behind the wheel of a car and driving is a different thing. Embrace the experiences, feelings and thoughts that you have inside yourself, doing so brings power to your life.

4th Path: Let Pain, Suffering, and Challenges Define You.

You are the sum of all your experiences. *~DeShawn Kenner*

The bottom line is that you cannot ever really win if you do not compete. Whether it's a spelling bee, Jeopardy, a race, fight, or sometimes love, on any level you must compete to move on to the next level. Like it or not we are all at odds with ourselves at some point. The first war that is waged in our lives is against one's self. We battle our own ignorance of not knowing in order to know how to survive, communicate, interact, eat, learn more, and hopefully mature more. This battle never stops, because the world we live in is always changing, and new improved methods and ways of doing things that enhance the quality of our lives become available.

In order to keep upgrading ourselves we must keep facing and accepting the challenges of learning, and new understandings that at times are not easily grasped. Your life can seem lonely, helpless, and overwhelmingly confusing and disorganized. It can seem like it hurts for no reason or for every reason. Know these are obstacles that all of mankind feels in an effort to progress. In the case of exercising, when done extensively and intensely the body gets tired and sore with muscle aches and pains. Yet at the same time when the body is rested, nourished properly with the right food, drinks, vitamins, and minerals the body not only grows but gets stronger. As it is with your life, which is constantly and consistently working with little to no rest because the world we live in is very demanding and is always forcing you to do something.

When you are mentally hurting or suffering those may be signs that you are growing and maturing mentally. No more than growing pains, like a new tooth coming in, new thoughts, ideas, and perspectives are entering into your mindset, it may seem like prolonged pain and suffering at times, but growth and development are always well worth it. Just like accomplishing something that you started, the competition with yourself is ongoing. Strive to outdo yourself, make your next move your best move always. The harder or smarter you work in your life the more rewards you will gain. There may come a time when the entire struggle you have endured will level off, and will become unnecessary because you will have mastered your craft, skill, and self. Always let the truths of self enlighten you, and never drive you crazy.

Power comes from overcoming and conquering what was once difficult. Do what is difficult until it becomes an effortless habit. At some point one has to stop crawling and start walking, however the crawl prepares you for the walk. Just like the walk prepares you for the run. The pain of resistance builds muscle and endurance. Keep innovation, renovation, maturation possible, and continue advancing.

5th Path: Silence, Hear Yourself Out

I couldn't hear myself until everything fell silent; then my voice became crystal clear. ~DeShawn Kenner

The two principal ways to regain ones balance in the midst of chaos and confusion is one to be still and two be silent. If a person feels disoriented for any reason to the point where everything seems to be spinning out of control and dizzy, that person should stop, simply sit, and be still. This way they cut the risk of falling, being seriously or fatally injured from walking, or stumbling into a dangerous situation, like oncoming traffic. Now to sit and be still is a start but not all that is required, because even though the physical senses may be off, what is really confused and thrown off is the mind. When the mind is not receiving adequate messages, is when the real disarray disorientation and panic set in.

The mind is the number one representative of oneself; it is directly connected to the heart, the physical body, and all its senses. When all these senses are understood by you through your mind and thoughts, one can begin to develop what is known as the sixth sense. Intuition, forethought, the third eye of seeing things unseen abstractly, and what is to come or what should be. The mind in essence is your third eye of seeing, with superior sight. So when the mind is disoriented or overloaded with nonsense, false perceptions, or too many outside influences; you are then disconnected on different levels. The mind from the self, anxiety, depression, the claustrophobic feeling of things closing in all around you leaving no room to breathe, are all directly connected. When these feelings and disconnections take place you are off balance, not just physically but also mentally with the spiritual self. When this happens you need quiet time, silence, and to be alone in order to reset yourself in all its functions. The silence filters out all the distractions and

noise pollution that you have been subjected to.
Once all the external interference has been
blocked out, your reception through all of your
mental and physical waves start to come back.
With the outside interference and interception
shut down, it is very important to develop very
strong connections and receptions with the self,
the mind, and the physical body. Especially in
regards to dealing with the external world and all
the different forces and energies that come with
it. From nature, animals, and other humans who
may have different mind sets and energy than you
do.

Whether it be in a wicked or good way,
sometimes a good fool is more dangerous than a
wicked Wiseman, although a wicked Wiseman
may consciously seek to do something malicious
and evil, the wicked Wiseman may use the
unknowing ignorant good fool to do it. Staying
firmly attached to the self, the mind, the heart, all
the physical senses, and emotions in every way
securely, cuts your risk dramatically of ever being
the good fool and even the wicked Wiseman.

When the self is completely balanced and governing all the systems of self properly, the real in tuned self will not allow wisdom, knowledge, or understanding to be improperly used or abused. The self that sees and understands with complete clarity and without distraction, with complete control over all functions of self will not allow any parts of the whole to be run over, ruled unjustly, disrespected, or to even move about disrespectfully. The respect for self begets respects from others and always from you.

In those moments of silent retreat with self, reinforce your reality, and objectives of your mind, body, and other functions. Never allow your mind to lose sight, touch, feel, or voice of self. All outside invasions and influences should always in some way be acknowledged and brought to the attention of the complete self in its unified, coexisting, intertwined manner. However nothing should overwhelm you to the point where you lose control, connection, or reception with yourself. In the den of silence, self and senses bind them in a covenant bond that cannot ever easily be broken, if broken at all.

Hear and feel the true majesty of self speak, I'm going to add another element to this silent retreat with self, there is nothing like the spoken word. Just like a singer or bird must let the beauty of their self and soul out into the physical world for all to hear, it must let the melody out first and foremost so that it can enjoy the beauty, song, energy, and truth of its own self. Do not be afraid to speak your truths or thoughts out into the world of reality. Know if you can feel your own truths or ideas of them, because the truth is not something that has to be seen, but something that has to be felt. If you can't feel your own truth, reasoning, or logic, who else should? Contrary to popular irrational belief, there is absolutely nothing wrong with reasoning with yourself and answering the sovereign of self, you. Like I said in 'No More Mistakes" if you cannot talk to you, then you will have a tough time talking to anyone else.

I believe the deception about not talking to self was started by some wicked Wise men whose aim was to control the minds and thoughts of the masses. They probably said something to the effect of, 'if you talk or listen to yourself you are crazy, so listen to me. What I have to say to you is much better than what you can say to yourself, because what you say or think makes no sense. Let me do all the thinking and you do what I say.' That's probably how kingdoms and organized religions were started. Not to say that it has all done bad, however in modern times people much prefer democracy and the freedom to choose over absolute ruler ship and dictated choices. Which do you prefer? However I must say this, in order for civilization to keep expanding in its greatest most mature capacity, each individual needs to be growing and expanding in their individual greatest most mature capacity. Every person is a pixel that is part of a bigger picture, and together at our finest most mature individual selves, when working together create a high definition view. The sense, relationship, and bond that you have with yourself should be so unshakable, so unbreakable, so solidified, that all you can end up as with self is a great understanding Wiseman.

The silence, solutions, and security of self
cultivate this power when taken seriously and
done consciously. It is said that nothing is louder
than silence, that's because you can finally hear
yourself and all of your thoughts, heart, and
feelings. Don't resist, hear yourself out, and hear
yourself speak. When someone is said to be
talking gibberish in front of an audience,
someone may ask the speaker, 'do you hear
yourself?' Insinuating that the speaker did not
even take the time out to hear their own self out
before they delivered it to that audience. Make
sure you are on point with yourself or with your
vocals metaphorically speaking before you step
out on to that stage, fine tune.

When I was a kid I might have spelled word five
or ten times out loud or until it registered deep in
my brain and etched into written stone on the
rock in my mind. Not to mention all the phone
numbers I had to recite to myself until I could
write them down. The mind, the memory, and
the brain feel them focus and function, deep

in the confines of yourself, in the humbleness of silence. It is a beautiful thing and an extraordinary strength to have.

When you know who you are nobody can tell you who you are. If you can sit with yourself in silence and be comfortable with you, then you have discovered your allegiance and friendship with yourself. First and foremost you should be your first, most loyal, loving, and trusted ally. You should under any circumstance be the most comfortable with you in your own skin where you really reside. You should always have your own back no matter what situation may occur. Let there be peace within you, understand that silence is holy. A place to reconcile, atone, and set the tone, do not be afraid of the silence. It exists for a reason, to groom you not to doom you. Fortify yourself, mature, and grow yourself through silent times. With all the invading and overwhelming forces of nature and mankind at play that may more often than not seem deeply oppositional to your position. You will always need a deep rooted sense of self to keep yourself grounded, balanced, and pushing forward through tremendously dense resistance to where you stand. You must know yourself and know yourself well, and trust you with your own life.

The offense, defense, and advancement of your own life is of paramount importance. If you wish to help someone else, you must be in some way able to help yourself. If you cannot help yourself, then you cannot help anyone else, except for maybe the wicked Wiseman that is always looking for a few good fools. Take a moment of silence for what was just said. Remember silence is very powerful. If you do not have peace with yourself you cannot have true peace with anyone else.

6th Path: Recognize When Things are not the Same

It used to be difficult to tell when a laugh turned into a cry, but not anymore. ~DeShawn Kenner

This is a very extraordinary power that will always keep you three steps ahead of the crowd. There are always indicators that a new season is about to begin. Just like the autumn sets up for the winter or the spring sets up for the summer. Life gives you signs of the new day to come. When you have decided to be honest, interrogated, and embraced yourself; accepted the challenges, pains, sufferings, and have stood face to face with them fearlessly; and have sat in silence hearing yourself out; then you can recognize when things are not the same. Things have changed not only in the plain view of the world, but also in the not so easily seen internal world of yourself.

Let me say before I go any further, that the changes which are always occurring in our societies, countries, and immediate surroundings first take shape and develop within the mind of a person. Everything stems from imagination, vision, creative thought process, which are triggered by the physical needs and wants of the human body. For instance no matter how spoiled, self centered, or egotistical a person may be, that person can agree with and accept the fact that nature, natural disasters, and all of its seasons do not and will never change for anybody. We must conform to the changes of temperature and climate that nature sees fit to dispense. In addition the need of the body must be met on the basic level of food and water. The fundamental needs of every person is food, water, heat, clothes, shelter, oxygen, and security; because we all must be safe from danger if we are going to survive. On any level a person had to realize when their needs change. When it is 90 degrees outside with the humidity to match, shorts and a tank top with a spot in the shade, and some lemonade; may be what you need to be doing. Even better would be to be in the house underneath the air conditioning. In contrast if it were ten degrees below zero there would be a need for long johns, thick socks, boots, coats, pants, and sweaters will be in need if outdoors. While indoors a fireplace or heating system of any type will be mandatory and blankets. We can equate these needs to survival. Just like growing and harvesting corn, wheat, rice, potatoes, fruits, and vegetables; or catching fish and the possible slaughtering of animals are necessary for food for the body to function. Some people do not like the fact that animals are eaten or that trees are cut down; but regardless of how they feel they must pick a source of protein, some carbohydrates, and other vitamin and mineral sources to eat, if they want to continue living. Like it or not it is the raw reality.

As it is so with the times, relationships and interests that a person has may change, you must know when the time has come for you to step up or fall back in any situation. The children who were once taken care of by strong adults will become the strong adults taking care of the next generation of children and aging elders. When mom can no longer see as well as she used to, dad can no longer lift things like he once could, or they have difficulty with their memory; then it is time for you to step up, that is power. If you are a cold, selfish person with no sense of compassion for your own not only in the nuclear family sense but in the "it takes a village" point of view, there will be part of responsibility always lacking and a piece of your strength always missing too. Unless a parent has done to you unthinkable wrongs, there is no excuse for abandonment. Just like the parent or guardian has to know when it is time to give the child, teenagers, or young adult space to grow. When a youngster is able to take on tasks such as cleaning up behind themselves, doing their homework without being told to, or just being respectful because it is the right thing to do. This yougin' deserves respect equally because they have given it freely and have shown maturity.

As I said before internal changes precede external changes. When you are in tune with yourself it will show externally through that mood that behavior. If you are in a good mood internally your physical actions will display that. Your disposition towards other people will be friendly and more helpful. Whereas if you are in an angry place with yourself for any reason, whether it be fear or confusion, which will show in your physical actions; ways this will show are being confrontational, belligerent, or passive aggressive. The place that we are within ourselves literally creates the world that we live in.

Whenever mankind began to roam the planet and came up against all of mother nature's elements, at some point man consciously realized that they had to make certain moves in order to survive. Whether it was to learn to make and set traps for food, to make tools to hunt, or skin animals for their hides and fur for cold winters. Learn to plant and harvest food to save for droughts and winters, to make shelter, or manipulate the elements in order to have in the event there was not enough. In any event man has always had the ability to recognize when his needs have changed and things for whatever reason were no longer the same.

With the self psychologically and emotionally those tasks still exist. You can outgrow a situation, a person, and you only hurt yourself by staying in that particular situation, person, or group, especially if the scenario is negative. Imagine when you were in elementary school despite all of your accomplishments in the sixth grade, you never moved on to the next grade. Imagine being stuck right there for the next fifteen or twenty years. Just going over the same material. Where would the growth and development be in that? Confined to a level that you had dominated long ago. You must know when it is time to move on, trade the horse in for a car, because there are freeways everywhere.

When a child is young more often than not the child plays with the other children from the neighborhood that their parents decided to move into. Goes to the schools that their parents see fit to send them to or that the district determines based on location or some other factor. To some great degree when you're young, you have limited options over whom you will associate with. You will have to go where you are told, and deal with whoever is in that environment or class. When a person is growing and maturing mentally with self, they realize at some point that they do not have to deal with everybody in that environment just because they are there sharing space. Nor is there a need for violence because no associations are formed. When a person becomes aware of this truth deep within the self, they can be said to be of a different more evolved self and psychology. You connect with people who are of like minded, a kindred spirit, of the same spirit, or energy. You won't try to fit into any particular group because it is thought that if you are in that circle then you are in the loop or will be more popular. Especially when you might not like any member of that group. You might not be able to identify with any of them as far as intellect or interest is concerned, you won't get caught up in the false image of prestige.

When you truly understand and know these facts, you will have obtained a spiritual liberation, a freedom within self, and freedom is power. A democracy to choose what you want to do and see how you want to see, through the eyes and mind of your truths, to exist in any form freedom is a must. If the freedom to breathe is taken away, a person will suffocate and die. If the heart loses its independent freedom to beat a person will drop dead, so freedom in some form must remain untouched. Especially in its most precious forms of the mind, heart, self, and breathing air. When a person recognizes these things they also recognize when things are not the same and that all things are subject to change. Some things change just to stay the same, like an apple tree bearing an apple seed to become someday another apple tree to take its place, in the unfortunate event it cannot survive. Even nature recognizes that things can change often and is always in the process of rebirth.

We must also be reborn, through levels in life

from immaturity into maturity, from ignorance into excellence, and from a hard head into an open mind. Through these rebirths of the self and mind comes a released power that even strengthens the body, because the self understands how vital and key the physical frame is to this physical world, and how our physical corresponds to the physical world. The body has laws on how much it can take and do those also need to be recognized. That fact has allowed the self and mind to come up with solutions for our own physical handicaps, we cannot physically fly so we build jets. We cannot swim an ocean with all our belongings on our back so we build huge ships that can. We must know our limits, so we can create ways to surpass them. For that one reason we must always recognize changes, because that is power!

7th Path: The Ruler, Teacher, Student, Servant

I stand here before you not as a prophet but as a humble servant of you, the people. ~Nelson Mandela

At the square root of all people there are four main character traits of the self: the ruler, the teacher, the student, and the servant. Let us not confuse or place negative connotations on the word servant, let us define what it is versus what it is not. Let's start with the word slave, which is an abused servant. No one on any level should be abused, humiliated, or embarrassed to the point where they feel like a slave, a fool, or a disgrace to themselves or other people for any rational valid reason at all. Who wants to feel or be portrayed in such a way? Nobody. The ruler, teacher, student, and servant are in essence one and the same within self. They are the four corners of the self which is each represented by a perfect ninety degree angle, which creates the complete square. The ruler, teacher, student, and servant have and make up endless combinations, just like bitter, sweet, sour, and spicy make up endless flavor combinations.

The ruler although the dictator must be a great servant on any level with self or with their ruled class. This is evident in many ways, a person may rule their own self, however they see fit, and it should be beneficial to the self as well. When one eats, drinks, bathes, or even uses the bathroom, one must clean the self which is serving the self. A person can be as hard and ruthless on the self as they would like, but they still have to serve themselves in the end. Naturally the self enjoys this, because it knows better than anyone else what it likes and considers serving the self a very intimate and private act, not to be exploited. Even if a ruler has a public and they are not serving them well, they run the risk of being overthrown or not re-elected. Many governments have been overthrown because they did not serve their people correctly, if at all. America for example, rebelled against British rule and gained her independence from the British Monarchy because the people residing in America were not being served and were being treated poorly by their ruling class. King Henry the 8th of France was beheaded by a public that did not feel he was serving correctly, so they felt betrayed.

I have already talked about the importance of a ruler being a servant; however a great servant makes a great teacher because they give education. They provide knowledge, wisdom, and understanding. A true great ruler is always a student of his self or people, learning always what the people want and need, as well as what the self wants and needs. A great student will become a great teacher and the great teacher was a great student first. If people look to seek the great teacher for counsel, guidance, and strategy then likewise the great teacher is the ruler because the people seek the direction of the leader.

The student is vital in correlation to the leader,

the teacher or servant, because while learning the student's main purposes are the studies of life. In order to become a great teacher the student must be proficient in these studies in order to evolve into the ultimate teacher and ruler.

So as above, so is below being the ultimate servant is the same as being the ultimate ruler. The paramount purpose of the ruler is to be a selfless servant of the people, which in this case is the self. In other words learning how to serve yourself, learning to attain lessons from yourself, to grow and teach yourself, all are in an effort to become the most profound ruler of self you can be.

If any of these four traits of the self is suppressed or blocked for whatever reason then the self is off of its square so to speak. The main thing that keeps the self off its square and incomplete is false pride. Too proud or egotistical to serve the self, let alone someone else, fear of leading, teaching, and learning. When engulfed in these types of fears, a person can only deteriorate into slave like behavior. Where the disrespect for leading, teaching, and learning is so egregious that the self feels subservient and others see you as a worthless thing that deserves no respect at all, worse than an animal.

The power of connecting these four corners of self is intense and tremendous. In order to release this strength one must not be fearful or so ignorant that they see leading, teaching, learning, or serving as a negative thing, or beneath their own capacity to do. In order to gain this majestic power, one must be humble enough to be aware of and accept one's own shortcomings or lacking. It is a good thing to be proud when something of goodness or greatness is accomplished. However to be proud in the sense of being excessively arrogant to the point where a person is always being degrading or condescending, puts the strength of the four corners off. To be the most excellent leader, one must also be the most excellent teacher, student, and servant. The truth is you can put them in any order you like, they all correspond perfectly on any level.

The power of self when connected internally,

*

projects itself out into the physical world. The greatest achievements and accomplishments of mankind are born when this happens, because it inspires others and ignites them at the core of themselves, just as one lit candle can light another. It is the substance that religions, political, and national movements are made of. For positive or negative reasons, regardless of the outcomes to date. Whether it spawned the movements of Judaism, Islam, Christianity, or the beginning of Pharaohs which in turn had pyramids built and the earliest civilizations established. The connection of the four corners of self even gave men such as Nelson Mandela, Napoleon Bonaparte, Adolf Hitler, Moses, Fidel Castro, George Washington, Leonardo DaVinci, Mother Teresa, Jesus Christ, The prophet Muhammad, and Alexander the Great the capabilities to manifest their visions and leave their mark on history. We are not going to focus on right or wrong or the adverse effects these people's movements may have had on others. What we are focusing on is their individual but equal ability to lead, teach, learn, and serve, without fear for their perspective groups, religions, cultures, colors, and nations. I have gone through different eras and ages just to show how far apart and different they may seem, but all operated with the same functions of leading, teaching, learning, and serving. The people provided these functions not just to themselves but their own people from which they grew. Some of this list had more flaws and ruthlessness than others, which in the more enlightened age of today we are still learning from and tweaking.

The science of today has proven that regardless of the physical outward appearances determined by our DNA, where we are from and the different accents this may produce, and our differences in gender and blood types, that all human beings are basically the same. We all share the same desires to be safe, have food, be healthy, have water, fresh air, and be warm. We also share similar aspirations, dreams, motives, emotions, and potential to connect all four corners of self and become complete, all of us!

With all this power at our fingertips what keeps

mankind so divided and split up? What keeps the selves of us all at odds even though we have common goals and interests? We all exist technically of the same substance and race, the human race! It is the subject of our next path to power. Why even though the self can connect and release unlimited power, we have yet to get a bull's-eye shot that benefits all of humanity and not just fragments of people at different times.

8th Path: Acknowledging the Methods, Ideas, and Ideals that Keep the Self and Others Separated

It's funny how you can cross the street and be in a whole other world. ~DeShawn Kenner

The perfect square of self may be aligned, however the methods, ideas, and ideals of how a person will lead, teach, learn, and serve varies. These corners come in many different styles with the self and selves of others; which brings about resistance, confusion, and conflict with the self and others. What has been said is lust, hate, envy, and jealousy keep the self and others at odds. I am going to articulate what I see keeping the self and mankind at odds.

1) Religion: 'Mine is better than yours.' Many men women, and children have been murdered in the name of countless religions.

2) Complexions: I'm black, I'm white, I'm brown, etc.

3) Nationalities: I'm American, I'm German, I'm Jamaican, I'm Haitian, I'm Dominican, I'm Puerto Rican, etc. This even breaks down further into the state, city, town, and block 'I'm from 3rd Ave.'

4) Sex: Men and boys become secret or outright enemies over a female one or both like, and females do the same vice versa for a male they like. Almost like a natural competitive instinct kicks in, a very powerful divider.

5) Money: Everything between friends, family, lovers, or associates are cordial until the money element is introduced and greed rears its ugly head.

6) Drugs: Controlled substances tend to bring the worst out of people. If the user can not afford that get high there is no telling how low a person will go to get high. Drug abuse in the twenty-first century has shown us all that.

7) Same Sex Preferences: Even though the government enforced laws in many countries to protect gay rights, lots of people still cannot accept it.

8) The Alpha Syndrome: This is when a person just wants to dominate or rule others by aggression, manipulation, or any means necessary; with or without consent which causes resentment, hostility, and

conflict. They also feel they are better because for example they are taller, stronger, shorter, smarter, etc.

9) Languages: Every language of every culture and subculture bring division, because there are too many meanings, definitions, and dialects at play. Most of the people who speak their particular style of talk, crown their communication system as the best which causes confusion and conflict.

10) Ignorance: Just not knowing and in some cases not wanting to know better. Thinking that you or we are that much different from them, when we actually are not.

11) Beliefs/Traditions: Many are ancient or outdated that stem from a time when most humans were still very superstitious, illiterate, and uneducated. Once they

thought the world was flat, believed the Sun revolved around the Earth, or as written into the US Constitution that all Black people of people of African descent were 3/5 human (although later remedied in the 13th Amendment). Still to this day many fixed outdated traditions still hold more weight than sound scientifically, rationally reasoned, evidence supported facts, and truths. Prime example Christopher Columbus discovered North America, which is still a holiday even though this is false. These become psychological holds which can be very strong and difficult to break.

12) Power Struggle: everybody wants to be the toughest, smartest, and most influential bar none, this keeps most at odds in some way.

13) Government Styles: Capitalism, Democracy, Communism, Socialism, Laissez-Faire, etc.

14) Selfish Greed: Person only thinks about one's own self regarding gaining or having anything, and wants everything the way they want it and for just them.

I'll speak on the selfish greed briefly. If you have ever needed help for anything from learning your ABC's, how to speak the language, being protected from danger, being fed when hungry, or been given a drink when thirsty; then having experienced any of these situations or dilemmas should be reason enough for you to check your own selfish greed. It does not matter that selfishness and greed are natural occurrences in every human being, because it is natural for a person to want to save their own life and feed their own hunger. Humans have other characteristics such as compassion, empathy, sympathy, love, hate, envy, jealousy, and intelligence; which are all very strong forces in a person as well. Every person has these good and bad qualities in them.

Civilization and the world would cease to exist if we did not in some way work together and take care of one another. The strongest most intelligent men and women can get sick or hurt and nobody wants to be left for dead or without some type of help. No one person is a continent or an island, even the most selfish and greedy people need a hand sometimes. Also check your selfish greed, if we all thought exclusively with selfish greed we would not survive, because we would all double cross and kill each other.

The human race could get so much more accomplished if we would stop going against each other for any made up reason to do so. United we stand, divided we fall. One planet, one people, one purpose, which is to progress. Understand this wisdom about self and others and you will see how petty and frivolous the things that separate mankind are. You will instantaneously experience a mental evolution, an awakening which is the essence of pure power.

The mind is the third eye. Once the mind is open and seeing with clarity, then the world you see through your physical eyes will see the world in its real way and no longer a distorted view.

We can share and have the best methods, ideas, and ideals without snaking or turning on each other. In order to establish a more proficient world, be wise enough to know when to let someone else take the lead. Once again keep this in mind; one planet, one people, one purpose, to progress. With having said that let's focus on our next path to power.

9th Path: Purpose and Progress

There's more to life than being born to die. ~*DeShawn Kenner*

I have already established that we live on one planet, we are one people, we have one purpose, which is to progress. This path is geared towards purpose and progress because it is evident that we live on one planet (Earth), and we are one people (human beings, the human race). Purpose and progression belong to each individual person who then comes together with other individuals and forms the bigger picture. Looking at it from this stand point as I stated earlier, each individual can be seen as a pixel which is a piece of a picture that literally forms part of the bigger picture.

You may ask yourself what is your purpose in the progression? Progression is ongoing in all ways, always. You were born a baby who could not walk, talk, reason, or defend yourself from harm. As you were taught, your body matured, and your mind matured; you were able to start walking, talking, thinking reasonably and typically able to fend for yourself. That is and was progression.

Humans went from living in the wild to civilities and living in homes of all sorts. We went from rubbing sticks and twigs together to get fire, to having unlimited lighters and matches that produce fire instantly at our desire. We went from cooking over open fires to cooking on/in stoves, ovens, and microwaves. We went from hunting for all our food in the wild to food shopping and bargain hunting in superstores. From primitive sports to sophisticated sports such as the NFL and NBA. We went from walking barefoot at all times to walking in shoes of all kinds. I won't focus too much on the weapons progression, but we went from sticks and stones to guns and bombs. From needing a house phone or pay phone to having smart phones that always instantly connect us to everything. As you can see progression is always in session.

My question is what will be your purpose in progression, because everything is progress? It is up to you to discover your purpose, many times others help us do this by telling us things like 'you always are so good at that,' often 'that' which come naturally and we enjoy sharing freely with others is our purpose. Sometimes people can see more clearly what you are good at or gifted in, because they are looking from the outside in. It is the equivalent of standing on top of a roof, looking down at the crowd versus being in the mix of the crowd. The person on the roof has a clearer view of everything happening around the person than the person in the crowd does. In order to accept this view from someone they must be trusted by you and wise.

At the same time you must be able to take a step back mentally to see if what is going on with yourself. Through paths such as silence and interrogation to reflect on where you stand and are at any given time, because in the end your view of self is most important. Purpose varies from person to person. A can opener and can are just as valuable as a scarf or buttons on a shirt. A bike has been as useful as a train has. The computer has been a breakthrough just as the internet, television, radio, an elevator, and this list goes on. Humans male and female of all the eras of all ages have created and done purposeful things that have helped advance our world. Everyone who has contributed has not been as recognized or famous as a Benjamin Franklin, Bill Gates, Mark Twain, or George Washington Carver. The number of people who have made our world more comfortable to be in is countless.

Find a purpose or purposes and add on to the progression of our world nation. Any and all fields count from an educator, engineering, plumbing, electrician, farming, masonry, computer technicians, nurses, doctors, inventors, garbage collectors, janitors, lawyers, firemen, scientists, politicians, religious figures, parents, or a helper of any sort there is no purpose too small or too big. Everything counts towards progression!

There may be purposes not mentioned that you will control, create, manage, or just help with. Not everything we do should be with the expectation of compensation either. Money is good incentive but not necessary for progression. If there was no money to be made or exchanged we would not just drop dead, stop surviving or building to protect ourselves from all the elements of nature, to feed and clothe ourselves, or to make the quality and standards of living better for ourselves; because it is what we are naturally capable of doing. Just living forces us all to make moves to maintain ourselves or we will all die. We naturally fight or resist death and suffering. Survival always has and always will be mankind's greatest motivation to progress with purpose. Money is just a good incentive to actually do what we should be doing anyway.

Money is actually an illusion that does not really exist. It is created by man and given a meaning. If the government says money is valid it is valid (fiat). Just like holidays, Christmas is more associated with Santa Clause and gift giving than it is with Jesus Christ at this point. Bottom-line is that people give words meaning, deeds meaning, and traditions meaning. Green means go and red means stop, because that is what man has decided it will mean in regards to traffic lights and accounting. You can give definition and meaning to your own purpose. You can change the game, the world with your purpose and help bring the world to a higher level. Use your mind, imagination, creativity, and physical capabilities to project our world and future forward and up.

What I am about to say is very important; do not spend your time learning countless facts and truths only to become a smart idiot or a wicked Wiseman. There are countless people on our planet who have the capability through strength, understanding, and wisdom to push our planet towards perfection, yet they do nothing with their talents and skills. Some go into gangs and meaningless street wars killing and harming for virtually nothing. While some are playing knockout games, knocking out old ladies for fun.

Some walk around spitting game all day, with the finest words, just to get over or con somebody.

What troubles me is that if you talked to just about most notorious gangsters, street level thugs, drug dealers, pimps, prostitutes, thieves, even rapists or pedophiles; most have a great deal of common sense, charisma, and intelligence. They can give you an ends justifies the means rationale. I say any person who can give rationale for these types of things is either a smart idiot or a wicked Wiseman.

A smart idiot is a person who is stupid or ignorant and they do not really realize that they aren't being smart at all. The wicked Wiseman may be so bent on their own selfish greed that they will turn away from the justice of a situation just to get what they want at whatever expense. The wicked Wiseman more often then not uses the smart idiot to do their dirty work. The wicked Wiseman knows that the smart idiot is really an idiot that thinks he is wise.

Remember the Wiseman can play the fool but the

fool can never play the Wiseman. In the same manner the wicked Wiseman can play the smart idiot but the smart idiot can never play the wicked Wiseman. The wicked Wiseman is capable to use anyone ignorant, good, bad, or not in tune with the self.

It is up to you to check your motives and means for your end results. That is the difference between the Wiseman and the wicked Wiseman. The things they will and will not do to obtain their end results, even if both have the same purpose and end goal. Whether a person is aggressive or deceitful necessarily or unnecessarily makes the difference. Use your knowledge, understanding, and wisdom for your purpose and progression wisely. Help another to find their wisdom and purpose if possible, because it is all in the name of progress.

Politicians, religious figures, law enforcement agents, doctors, and educators of any type are not excluded from being capable of being able to be wicked wise men. They can be the wickedest wise men. Selfish greed and power tripping can take over anyone if not checked. Being wise, having purpose and progressing are very powerful forces, which require a great deal of responsibility and maturity. It is time to grow up in self, milk for babies and meat for men is what old wisdom said, and I agree.

They say you cannot change who you are, but with a clear understanding of yourself you can definitely change the poor choices you can make into the best decisions possible.

10th Path: Conquering Complexes of the Self

Make you easier to love by loving yourself first. ~*DeShawn Kenner*

Complexes are things that a person may not like about themselves, which makes them feel inferior to another or others. Some may have short person complex, others tall person complex, others may not like their teeth, weight, or overall look. The list could go on for miles, this psychological hang-up keeps many people insecure. Over conscious of the physical self and stagnated as far as purpose and progression are concerned. This should not be the case, because the change that you will make will come from within yourself. Your spirit, your imagination, your leader, student, teacher, servant mentality, with your purpose and progression will make the

difference, your voice will make the difference.
Martin Luther King, Jr. was black in a time when
to the ruling majority was not cool, however that
man embraced his own skin and made a
difference. Napoleon Bonaparte was said to have
had a short man complex, but he overcame that
complex, lead France to victory and became a
ruler.

When complexes go unchecked, they can make
people unnecessarily hostile, violent, shy, timid,
or overbearing from too many unnecessary things
to prove. When the connection within yourself is
solid and secure you will understand that the
power you control and exude will radiate. This
radiates from within yourself and not from your
physical looks, your physical beauty is directly
connected to your inner beauty. It is a great thing
to take care of the physical self because it
represents you. If the physical model type beauty
was all that mattered to people, only beauty
pageant queens, pretty boys, the most attractive
men and women would rule the world and
control everything. This is not the case,

influential and life changing people come in all sizes, shapes, complexions, heritages, and not all of these people are attractive physically. These are just mastermind people whose leader, teacher, student, and servant corners of self have connected with purpose. That in and of itself is raw beauty that supersedes the physical appearance.

Think about a singer of any type who without uttering a melody may not appear that physically appealing at all, but upon hearing their beautiful, powerful voice, they took on a beauty that their physical body could not otherwise produce. It is a more unique distinctive type of beauty that the physical world cannot produce. It comes from the beauty within even if the voice is possessed by a wicked Wiseman. Your actions, how you carry yourself, how you treat other people, your level of respect for yourself and others is how you will genuinely be measured and viewed. Looks can and will change it is inevitable, but the character of a person is almost never forgotten. There are physically beautiful people all over the planet. Some of these people have attitudes and so unlikeable and nasty that they are unbearable to be around and because of their depressing dispositions become very unattractive to people that are around them. Remember the changes to life and joy you will give to the world will come from within and show outwardly.

If you are a good person with gorgeous physical looks, be humble about it. Do not go around looking down on people because you feel they are not as good looking, tall, short, light, or dark as you are. It is a wonderful thing to have good self esteem but it is a terrible thing to always be condescending and belittle people because of their looks in comparison with your own. What does that say about you, if you are only able to measure your worth or beauty against someone else's? A person, who truly knows beauty, sees or understands that beauty and power come in different forms. Just like the sun has its own power and beauty, so does the ocean, birds, bees, ants, elephants, flowers, and trees. Everything has its own unique power and beauty.

To those who feel like they do not measure up to someone else's standards of beauty, intelligence, or whatever other shortcoming that may exist, do not be hateful, envious, or jealous, because it will restrict your power. Just recognize your worth, value, and unique beauty, because when you do you will be able to release your own personal power.

11th Path: The Blame Game

The only person you ever truly have the right to blame is yourself.
~Sarah Anne

You must never indulge in the blame game, if you are ever to master your mind and self. You can never be a true leader or lead yourself if you do not take credit for your own actions and responsibility for your own decisions. Blaming someone else for a choice you have made is an indication of weakness. You cannot truly expect anyone to respect you by doing this, nor can you consider yourself an independent mature person by constantly being dependent on someone else to take the fall for your immature behavior or decisions.

A person who is aligned with all corners of self, who moves with purpose, who is honest with their self, who has embraced who they are, who has sat silently and reflected, who is a true leader, teacher, student, and servant, and can recognize when things are not the same and have changed, this person could never allow another or others to be credited with the decisions that they have freely elected. This is why it is so important to investigate and double check any choice you decide to make. The person who masters their self has too much self respect to allow anyone else to lay claim to their victories or failures, because they know they can never really lose. Even when they encounter a temporary lose, they learn valuable lessons so they still actually win.

The person with true power of self knows that their power grows with every experience successful or not as long as they consciously own those experiences and decisions. The blame game is lame and weak. Refraining from playing this game will ensure that you constantly maintain full control over yourself. Who better to have mastery and power over you than yourself? Blame no one for what you decide to do...

12th Path: Respect Yourself

Respect is an indicator of the commencement of change.
~DeShawn Kenner

This is a must for many reasons. I will start out with if you do not respect yourself, it will be impossible for you to respect anyone else. It is no secret that a person must give respect to get it in return. Regardless if others are respecting you or not the least you can do at all times is respect yourself. There are times when a person gives sincere respect and cannot receive it in return, because the other person may not even respect their self or is just being oppressive. An example of this type of oppression, what the Nazi Regime was to the victims of the Holocaust, the Jews.

Viktor Frankl was a Holocaust survivor who wrote a book about his very painful experience. The name of his book is 'Man's Search for

Meaning,' which I strongly recommend to read. This book is also about finding meaning in life and self discovery. Mr. Frankl explains regardless of how disrespectful and degrading Nazis were during that time, the one thing he maintained was his personal dignity and self respect. This was something that he truly owned and no one could take away from him. Always looking toward the future helped him stay focused.

When you respect yourself you cannot help but be honest with yourself, to lead, teach, learn, and serve yourself with the utmost respect, love, care, and concern. Once you establish respect and loyalty to yourself you can begin to give that to others. For instance if you cannot carry yourself, how can you carry anyone else? It is impossible! Everything begins with the self. An apple seed has to grow into an apple tree before it can grow apples which produce more seeds. A strong sense of respect for self inspires others to respect themselves which in turn breeds a mutual respect for all. Disrespect never goes unnoticed, especially with the self.

It is said that human beings at their core are just animals too. You as a human being are far from an animal. No animal as of yet has shown the intelligence, desire, or spirit to produce what the human or the human mind has created, visualized, or imagined. Day after day, year after year we out do ourselves on the levels of creativity and invention. You, I, we all have a responsibility and duty to our individual and collective intelligence, which entails that you must respect yourself. What are you able to accomplish when you desire to and apply yourself to any particular mission positive or negative? Yes I also say negative as well because the wicked Wiseman accomplishes a lot of their own selfish greedy needs and wants too, just at the expense of others. Nevertheless you should have enough respect for what mankind has achieved thus far.

Mankind has accomplished a lot with the help of violence and atrocities. This has left lots of people on the planet broken, misunderstood, and struggling for identity, acceptance within the whole group of humanity. This scenario continues to cause unnecessary hostility, ruthlessness, animosity, and misdirected anger among humans. It is to the point where some humans find it justified to be wild and dangerous in order to survive, not against animals such as lions and wolves, but against other men, women, boys, and girls.

We are at war, at odds with our own selves and others. Always trying to control our tempers, fears, and anxieties to no end, this can be a full time job within itself. How can a person or people reach their full unleashed potential and power under those conditions? A person cannot fully learn, focus, or think when they are stressed out. The stress internally consumes them, while keeping up outward appearances if they can even do that. Just because a person smiles does not mean they are happy.

We may all want to get along and have ambitions of unification. It seems like we do not have the slightest idea of how to do it. This is evident in the ongoing conflicts of people, religion, and law enforcement and how they have distinguished the plights of man. Only we ourselves can solve our human issues, not fear of violence or brutal attacks will change the hearts and minds of people. In most cases violence just makes it worse, because the vengeance and hate grows, blinding man's rationality or in reverse giving him a reason to continue on his war path.

Very bright people come together to form United Nation groups, hold summits to discuss strategies to come together as one people, to curb not just gun violence but all violence, that no one goes hungry, unclothed, unsheltered, control the spread of disease, yet our social problems still continue. I believe it is a lack of respect not just for self but overall each other. An old piece of wisdom says, 'he who wants peace let him be prepared for war.' It seems that mankind has decided to do endless killings, incarcerating, and policing in the name of peace. At the rate we are going we may all go extinct in the name of peace. Whether people are attempting to protect their neighborhood (as allegedly claimed by George Zimmerman who shot Trayvon Martin to death), town, state, country, religion, way of life, women, children, sons, and daughters; we all have reasons for remaining separate and disrespecting each other. It is an exhausting thing for the human race that slows up our progress as a whole. Lots of people are fine with people remaining divided, if it benefits them in some way or adds to their own comfort ability. If disaster hit they would grab the hand of anybody willing to pull them out of danger.

It is a great thing to be righteous but never be self righteous, as if your own causes, beliefs, or reasoning is the only things that matter, do not ever be that disillusioned or cocky. Evolution is what survives us all; if that is the case then children need to learn these lessons as soon as possible. As the late great Whitney Houston sung, 'I believe the children are the future.' They must capitalize off the mistakes of the elders, before they go sour or irretrievably into separation, violence, and corruption. It does not mean they will be soft pushovers without the ability to stand up for themselves, it means those people of greater understanding, will teach them the wisdom of reasoning, empathy, feelings, and solidarity. We live in a world community, where you can be anywhere in the world that is just a phone call, drive, flight, or internet click away. A child's mind goes from the ignorance and has the ability to learn from the ages one to one hundred. Mental maturity has no set age, so we are all children who should never stop learning, growing, or maturing with the self.

Respecting the Self adds to and completes the Twelve Paths of Power; however it is still not over...

End of the Twelve Paths, but Not the End of the Journey

We will progress together, even if it is only one mind at a time.
~DeShawn Kenner

The Twelve Paths are the fundamentals for the ongoing journey of life. Having the power of these Twelve Paths within yourself will ensure that you meet the challenges and obstacles that living will present to you, head on with winning results. All people on the planet Earth will have to deal with the adversity of growing, which can be painful just like a new tooth coming in. Our burden being to overcome the problems that we will have with self, others, and the world in general; that we are strong enough and confident enough to keep pushing forward, even against all odds. Also realizing that none of us are alone in this world, even though we might be under the deception that we are at times because of the pain, suffering, hopelessness, and desperation that we all feel at times.

The powers to be honest, silent, interrogative, to embrace you, to have purpose and progress, to connect the four corners of self, to respect self, to conquer your complexes, not to play the blame game, to recognize what keeps people separated, letting pain and challenge define instead of break you, recognition of when things are no longer the same; all this power serves to bring clarity to one's own mind. Pushing the cloud of disillusionment and deception away from one's own eyes, so you can see and understand what is really going on inside and outside of you. It is all very much connected, you cannot solve a problem if you cannot see it, feel it, hear it, smell it, or understand it. To know what is underneath or behind your refrigerator you have to move it to see the area.

It is imperative that you keep these twelve ways of power in mind as you move towards bettering yourself and the world we live in. Always keep them in mind and apply them as much as you need to.

In the words of the late, great rap artist Heavy D, 'I wish you a peaceful journey.'

Everyday wisdom for everyday people of every walk of life because one planet, one people, one purpose to progress.

ABOUT THE AUTHOR

DeShawn Kenner was born in Mount Vernon, New York 1978. He was a hard headed youth who took to the streets. He made many mistakes along his life's journey and hindsight is always 20/20. The author has been on a journey of self discovery for all of his life. He traveled through life's highs and lows in search of self. While doing so, DeShawn previously delivered to you his first book No More Mistakes Guide to Making Better Decisions.

Made in the USA
Middletown, DE
01 June 2021